To My Family

for being my pillars of strength, source of courage, for teaching me to how to learn from all our experiences and for being the compass on values throughout my leadership journey.

To all My Leaders

for being exemplary leadership role models, for taking risks and giving me opportunities, for setting me up to succeed and catching me if I was to fall, for always nudging me to go further and giving me wings to fly.

If I can see further than others,

it is because I have stood on the shoulders of giants before me"

Sir Isaac Newton

This book is dedicated to all the women around the world who are driven to a higher purpose in life and striving to be a better version of themselves everyday.

CONTENTS

0	Introduction	01
1	Starting the Journey of Leadership as a Woman	06
2	Balancing Work and Life	13
3	Networking Like a Pro	19
4	Making Decisions with Confidence	25
5	Developing and Leading Teams	31
6	Growing Your Career Against All Odds	37
7	Regional and Global Roles	43
8	Managing Stress at Work	49
9	The Future of Work for Women	55
10	Career Progression in the Childbearing Age	62
11	Planning Retirement for Women Leaders	69
12	Embracing Your Leadership Journey	76

INTODUCTION

Welcome to GLOW: A Guide to Leadership for Outstanding Women. If you're holding this book, it means you're ready to embark on a transformative journey. Whether you're a seasoned professional or just starting out in your career, this guide is designed to illuminate the path to exceptional leadership, tailored specifically for women navigating the complex landscape of today's corporate world.

When I first stepped into the realm of leadership, I was met with both excitement and uncertainty. I quickly learned that the journey to becoming a leader is not a straight or fixed path, but rather a winding road filled with challenges, triumphs, and invaluable lessons. My experiences, shaped by years of navigating global and regional roles, reporting to a diverse array of leaders, and facing both supportive and challenging environments, have taught me that leadership is as much about self-discovery as it is about guiding others. It is very personal indeed.

In GLOW, you will find a reflection of my journey, enriched by the experiences of many remarkable men and women leaders I've encountered along the way. I wanted to share these as concise nuggets of wisdom already distilled from deep insights of my experiences rather than stories. This is because throughout my leadership journey, that is what I always wished I had – wisdom, solutions, directions, in bullet points if possible, concise and brief, not novels, not laced with stories which took a lot of my already precious time to read through for self-help. "No frills or fluff" and straight to the point as one of my leader's always reminded us when we had something to say.

To all women leaders of the world, especially those in demanding fields like healthcare, law, engineering, finance, and banking, this book is for you. It's for the women who strive to excel, who balance multiple roles, and who seek to lead with grace and confidence.

My hope is that GLOW will serve as a beacon, guiding you through the challenges and joys of leadership. May it inspire you to embrace your unique strengths, build a network of support, and shine brightly in all your endeavors. Remember, your leadership journey is not just about reaching the top; it's about glowing at every step of the way.

So, let's embark on this journey together. Let's learn, and lead with brilliance. Welcome to GLOW.

GLOW

A Guide to Leadership for Outstanding Women

CHAPTER 1

Starting the Journey of Leadership as a Woman

"The most effective way to do it is to do it."

Amelia Earhart

Laying the Foundation

Starting a leadership journey as a woman involves navigating unique challenges and leveraging distinct strengths. The initial steps of this journey are crucial in shaping one's leadership style, building credibility, and setting the tone for future growth. There are numerous published reports that confirm women in leadership face higher scrutiny and often have to prove their competence more than their male counterparts. However, with determination, strategic planning, and the right support, women can carve out successful leadership paths.

Strategies for Early Leadership Success

Develop Self-Awareness: Understanding your strengths, weaknesses, values, and motivations is essential. Self-awareness allows you to lead authentically and build trust with your team. Tools such as the Myers-Briggs Type Indicator (MBTI) or StrengthsFinder can provide valuable insights into your leadership style and areas for development.

Seek Out Mentorship and Sponsorship: Mentors provide guidance, advice, and support, while sponsors actively advocate for your advancement. Identify leaders you admire and seek their mentorship. Additionally, build relationships with sponsors who can help open doors and provide career opportunities.

Build Your Network: Networking is a powerful tool for career advancement. Attend industry events, join professional organizations, and connect with peers and leaders in your field. Building a diverse network can provide valuable insights, opportunities, and support throughout your career.

Continual Learning and Development: Invest in your professional development by pursuing further education, attending workshops, and seeking out learning opportunities. Staying updated with industry trends and acquiring new skills will enhance your competence and confidence as a leader.

Embrace Challenges and Take Risks: Stepping out of your comfort zone and taking on challenging projects can accelerate your growth. Embrace opportunities that push you to develop new skills and demonstrate your capabilities. Remember, growth often happens outside of your comfort zone.

Advocate for Yourself: Assertiveness is key in advancing your career. Communicate your accomplishments, seek feedback, and ask for what you deserve, whether it's a promotion, raise, or new opportunity. Being your own advocate ensures that your contributions are recognized and rewarded.

Situational Advice

For Women in Male-Dominated Industries: Entering a male-dominated industry can be daunting.

Build alliances with other women and supportive men in your field. Advocate for diversity and inclusion initiatives and lead by example. Showcasing your expertise and contributing meaningfully can help break stereotypes and pave the way for other women.

For Women Balancing Career and Family: Balancing career and family responsibilities can be challenging. Prioritize time management and set clear boundaries to ensure a healthy work-life balance. Seek flexible work arrangements and leverage your support network to manage family commitments effectively.

For Young Women Leaders: Young women leaders may face scepticism due to their age. Focus on building credibility through competence and professionalism. Seek mentorship from experienced leaders and continuously invest in your development. Demonstrating maturity and expertise will help you gain respect and establish authority.

KEY TAKEAWAYS

Self-Awareness

Develop a deep understanding of your strengths, weaknesses, and values to lead authentically.

Mentorship and Sponsorship

Seek out mentors for guidance and sponsors to advocate for your advancement.

Networking

Build a strong and diverse professional network for support and opportunities.

Continual Learning

Invest in ongoing professional development to stay competitive and confident.

Embrace Challenges

Take on challenging projects and step out of your comfort zone to accelerate growth

Self-Advocacy

Advocate for yourself and ensure your contributions are recognized and rewarded.

Embarking on a leadership journey as a woman requires self-awareness, strategic planning, and resilience. By developing strong networks, seeking mentorship, continually learning, embracing challenges, and advocating for themselves, women can build successful and fulfilling leadership careers. The journey may be challenging, but with determination and the right strategies, women can thrive and inspire others to follow in their footsteps.

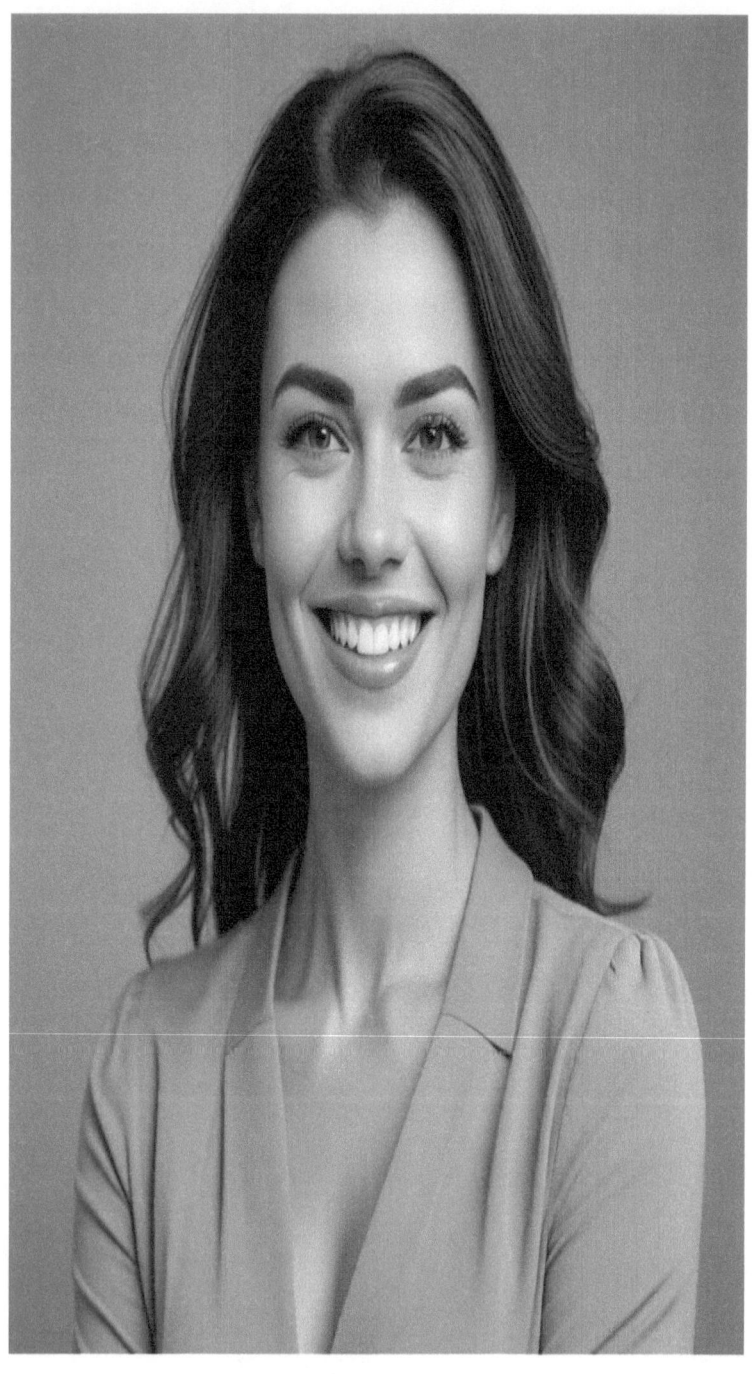

CHAPTER 2

Balancing Work and Life

"You cannot do it all. No one can have two full-time jobs, have perfect children, cook three meals, and be a superwoman till dawn... Superwoman is the adversary of the women's movement."

Gloria Steinem

Understanding the Challenge

Balancing work and life is a perpetual challenge for many leaders, but women often face unique pressures and expectations. From managing household responsibilities to navigating career progression, the balancing act can be particularly intense. This chapter explores the issues, pain points, and specific challenges faced by women worldwide and offers strategies and solutions to help them succeed.

Balancing work and life is not just about time management; it's about managing energy, setting boundaries, and prioritizing effectively. According to a Harvard Business Review article, women often experience greater levels of stress related to work-life balance compared to men. This can be attributed to societal expectations, unequal distribution of household responsibilities, and the pressure to excel in both professional and personal roles.

A study by McKinsey & Company found that women are more likely to experience burnout than men, with 42% of women reporting burnout compared to 35% of men. According to Pew Research, 60% of working mothers say balancing work and family is difficult.

Women often face societal pressure to be primary caregivers and excel in their careers simultaneously. This dual expectation can lead to significant stress and feelings of inadequacy when either role seems to fall short. Despite progress in gender equality, many women still bear a disproportionate share of household and caregiving responsibilities. This imbalance can hinder their professional growth and personal well-being. Furthermore, women leaders often feel the need to work harder to prove their competence and commitment, leading to overwork and burnout.

Strategies for Balancing Work and Life

Effective prioritization is crucial. The Eisenhower Matrix, a tool that categorizes tasks based on urgency and importance, can help you focus on high-impact activities. Time blocking, where you allocate specific time slots for different tasks, can create a structured routine that balances work and personal commitments.

Delegating tasks, both at work and home, can alleviate your burden. Engage in partnerships at home to share responsibilities and build a support network of family, friends, and colleagues. Reliable support systems are essential for managing stress and maintaining balance.

Establish clear boundaries between work and personal life. Avoid checking emails or taking work calls during personal time. Learning to say no to additional responsibilities that could overwhelm you is crucial.

Prioritize your well-being and focus on what truly matters.

Incorporate regular exercise and a healthy diet into your routine. Physical well-being significantly impacts mental health and productivity. Practice mindfulness and meditation to manage stress and maintain a positive outlook.

Situational Advice

For leaders managing global teams, use tools like World Clock to schedule meetings at mutually convenient times. Plan travel schedules efficiently to minimize time away from home and maximize productivity during trips.

For remote work, create a dedicated workspace at home to separate professional and personal life. Maintain a consistent daily routine to enhance productivity and balance.

For on-site roles, utilize commute time for personal growth activities like listening to audiobooks or podcasts. Negotiate flexible working hours, if possible, to better manage work and personal commitments.

> ## KEY TAKEAWAYS
>
> ### Prioritization
> Use tools like the Eisenhower Matrix and time blocking to prioritize tasks.
>
> ### Delegation
> Delegate tasks and build a strong support network.
>
> ### Boundaries
> Establish clear work-life boundaries and learn to say no.
>
> ### Self-Care
> Prioritize self-care through regular exercise, a healthy diet, and mindfulness

Balancing work and life is an ongoing process that requires intentionality and strategic planning. By prioritizing effectively, delegating tasks, setting boundaries, and focusing on self-care, women leaders can achieve a more harmonious balance and thrive in both their personal and professional lives.

CHAPTER 3

Networking Like a Pro

"Networking is not about just connecting people. It's about connecting people with people, people with ideas, and people with opportunities."

Michele Jennae

Understanding the Importance of Networking

Networking is a critical skill for any leader, but it holds special significance for women. Building a robust professional network can open doors to opportunities, provide support, and foster career growth. However, women often face unique challenges in networking, such as gender biases and limited access to high-level networks.

A study by LeanIn.Org and McKinsey & Company reveals that women are less likely than men to receive career-advancing networking opportunities. They often struggle to find mentors and sponsors who can advocate for them in professional settings. This lack of access can hinder career progression and professional development.

Women also face societal expectations that can make networking challenging. Traditional gender roles may discourage women from self-promotion and assertiveness, both crucial for effective networking. Additionally, balancing networking activities with personal and family responsibilities can be demanding.

Strategies for Effective Networking

Build and nurture relationships strategically. Identify key individuals in your industry or organization who can provide guidance, support, and opportunities. Attend industry conferences, seminars, and events to expand your network and stay informed about industry trends.

Leverage online platforms like LinkedIn to connect with professionals globally. Join professional groups and participate in discussions to increase your visibility. Regularly update your profile to reflect your achievements and expertise.

Seek out mentors and sponsors who can advocate for you. Mentors provide guidance and advice, while sponsors actively promote your career advancement. Be proactive in identifying and approaching potential mentors and sponsors.

Develop a personal elevator pitch that succinctly highlights your skills, experience, and career goals. This can help you make a strong impression during networking interactions.

Practice active listening and show genuine interest in others. Building meaningful relationships requires empathy and reciprocity. Offer help and support to others in your network, as this fosters mutual respect and trust.

Situational Advice

For those in global or regional roles, use video conferencing tools to maintain connections with your network. Schedule virtual coffee meetings or catch-ups to stay in touch despite geographical distances.

For on-site roles, participate in cross-departmental projects or committees to meet colleagues from different areas of your organization. This can expand your internal network and increase your visibility.

For remote workers, join virtual networking events and webinars. Engage actively in online communities related to your industry. Share your insights and experiences to establish yourself as a thought leader.

KEY TAKEAWAYS

Strategic Relationship Building

Identify key individuals and nurture relationships.

Online Networking

Utilize LinkedIn and other platforms to connect with professionals globally.

Mentorship and Sponsorship

Seek mentors and sponsors to guide and advocate for your career.

Elevator Pitch

Develop a concise pitch to effectively introduce yourself.

Networking is an essential skill that can significantly impact your career. By building strategic relationships, leveraging online platforms, seeking mentorship and sponsorship, and practicing active listening, women leaders can expand their professional networks and create opportunities for growth and advancement.

CHAPTER 4

Making Decisions with Confidence

"Do not bring people in your life who weigh you down. And trust your instincts—good relationships feel good. They feel right. They don't hurt."

Oprah Winfrey

Understanding the Decision-Making Challenge

Decision-making is a crucial aspect of leadership, and for women, it often comes with additional challenges. Women leaders may face gender biases that question their decision-making abilities. They might also experience self-doubt, influenced by societal expectations and stereotypes.

Research from INSEAD highlights that women are often perceived as less decisive compared to their male counterparts, despite evidence showing that women can be equally effective decision-makers. This perception can undermine their confidence and hinder their ability to make bold, strategic decisions.

Women also tend to experience higher levels of imposter syndrome, the feeling of being inadequate despite evident success. This can lead to hesitation and second-guessing, which affects decision-making.

Strategies for Confident Decision-Making

Understand and acknowledge the biases and stereotypes that may affect your confidence. Awareness is the first step towards overcoming these barriers. Challenge negative self-talk and replace it with positive affirmations.

Gather relevant information and data before making decisions. The Decision-Making Process, a model from Harvard Business School, suggests a systematic approach: identify the problem, gather information, evaluate alternatives, make the decision, and review the decision's impact. This structured approach can enhance confidence in your choices.

Build a supportive network of peers and mentors who can provide feedback and encouragement. Discussing your decisions with trusted advisors can offer new perspectives and reassurance.

Develop a habit of reflective practice. After making a decision, take time to reflect on the process and outcome. This can help you learn from your experiences and improve future decision-making.

Practice self-compassion. Accept that not all decisions will be perfect and that making mistakes is a part of the learning process. Be kind to yourself and focus on continuous improvement.

Situational Advice

For global or regional roles, consider cultural differences and time zone challenges when making decisions. Use collaborative tools to gather input from diverse team members and ensure inclusive decision-making.

For on-site roles, involve team members in the decision-making process to foster a sense of ownership and collective responsibility. This can enhance the quality of decisions and increase team engagement.

For remote work, leverage virtual collaboration tools to facilitate decision-making. Schedule regular check-ins with your team to discuss progress and address any challenges.

KEY TAKEAWAYS

Awareness
Understand and challenge biases and stereotypes.

Structured Approach
Follow a systematic decision-making process.

Support Network
Build a network of peers and mentors for feedback.

Reflective Practice
Reflect on decisions to learn and improve.

Self-Compassion
Embrace mistakes as learning opportunities.

Confident decision-making is essential for effective leadership. By understanding biases, following a structured approach, building a support network, practicing reflection, and embracing self-compassion, women leaders can make bold and impactful decisions with confidence.

CHAPTER 5

Developing and Leading Teams

"Leadership is not about being in charge. It is about taking care of those in your charge."

Simon Sinek

Understanding Team Development Challenges

Leading and developing teams is a fundamental responsibility for any leader. Women leaders, however, may encounter unique challenges in this area, such as gender biases, managing diverse teams, and balancing team needs with organizational goals.

A study by the Center for Creative Leadership found that women leaders often face scepticism about their leadership abilities, which can undermine their authority and effectiveness. Additionally, women may struggle with balancing assertiveness and empathy, two crucial traits for successful team leadership.

Women leaders might also face challenges in gaining the respect and trust of their teams, particularly in male-dominated industries. This can create additional pressure to prove their competence and effectiveness.

Strategies for Effective Team Development

Understand and leverage different leadership styles. The Situational Leadership Model by Hersey and Blanchard suggests adapting your leadership style based on the team's maturity and competence. This flexibility can enhance team performance and development.

Foster an inclusive and collaborative team culture. Encourage open communication, mutual respect, and diversity of thought. According to McKinsey & Company, diverse teams are more innovative and perform better.

Invest in team development through training and professional growth opportunities. Provide regular feedback and recognize team members' contributions. This can boost morale and foster a culture of continuous improvement.

Balance assertiveness and empathy. Assertiveness is necessary for setting expectations and holding team members accountable, while empathy is crucial for understanding and addressing their needs and concerns. Striking this balance can enhance your effectiveness as a leader.

Lead by example. Demonstrate the values and behaviours you expect from your team. Your actions can inspire and motivate your team members to emulate these qualities.

Situational Advice

For global or regional roles, consider cultural differences when leading diverse teams. Use inclusive communication practices and be mindful of different time zones when scheduling meetings.

For on-site roles, create opportunities for team bonding and collaboration through regular team-building activities. Foster a sense of belonging and shared purpose among team members.

For remote work, use virtual collaboration tools to maintain team cohesion and communication. Schedule regular virtual check-ins and team meetings to keep everyone aligned and engaged.

KEY TAKEAWAYS

Leadership Styles:
Adapt your leadership style to the team's needs.

Inclusive Culture
Foster a collaborative and inclusive team environment.

Team Development
Invest in training and recognize contributions.

Balance
Balance assertiveness with empathy.

Lead by Example
Demonstrate the values and behaviours you expect.

Developing and leading teams effectively requires understanding the unique challenges women leaders face, adapting leadership styles, fostering an inclusive culture, investing in team development, balancing assertiveness and empathy, and leading by example. By implementing these strategies, women leaders can build high-performing teams and drive organizational success.

CHAPTER 6

Growing Your Career Against All Odds

"If you're offered a seat on a rocket ship, don't ask what seat! Just get on it!"

Sheryl Sandberg

Understanding Career Growth Challenges

Growing a career in leadership is challenging, and women often face additional obstacles such as gender biases, lack of mentorship, and work-life balance issues. These challenges can impede career progression and create barriers to reaching senior leadership positions.

A report by LeanIn.Org and McKinsey & Company highlights that women are underrepresented in senior leadership roles, with women of colour facing even greater disparities. Women often have to work harder to prove their competence and gain recognition.

Imposter syndrome, a feeling of self-doubt despite evident success, is also prevalent among women leaders. This can undermine their confidence and hinder their career growth. Balancing career ambitions with personal and family responsibilities adds another layer of complexity.

Strategies for Career Growth

Set clear career goals and create a strategic plan to achieve them. Break down your goals into actionable steps and track your progress. Regularly review and adjust your plan as needed.

Seek out mentors and sponsors who can provide guidance, support, and advocacy. Mentors offer advice and feedback, while sponsors actively promote your career advancement.

Invest in continuous learning and professional development. Attend workshops, pursue certifications, and stay updated with industry trends. Enhancing your skills and knowledge can increase your value and open up new opportunities.

Build a strong personal brand. Clearly articulate your unique value proposition and consistently demonstrate it through your work. Use platforms like LinkedIn to showcase your achievements and connect with industry peers.

Network strategically. Attend industry events, join professional associations, and engage in online communities. Building a robust professional network can provide support, opportunities, and valuable insights.

Situational Advice

For global or regional roles, seek opportunities for cross-cultural learning and international assignments. This can broaden your perspective and enhance your leadership skills.

For on-site roles, take on challenging projects that showcase your abilities and drive career growth. Seek visibility by participating in high-impact initiatives and presenting your work to senior leaders.

For remote work, leverage virtual platforms to maintain visibility and build relationships. Regularly update your achievements and contributions on professional networks to stay relevant and connected.

KEY TAKEAWAYS

Career Goals
Set clear goals and create a strategic plan.

Mentorship
Seek mentors and sponsors for guidance and advocacy.

Continuous Learning
Invest in professional development.

Personal Brand
Build and showcase your unique value proposition.

Networking
Network strategically to expand your professional connections.

Growing your career as a woman leader requires setting clear goals, seeking mentorship and sponsorship, investing in continuous learning, building a strong personal brand, and networking strategically. By implementing these strategies, you can overcome obstacles and achieve your career ambitions.

CHAPTER 7

Regional and Global Roles

"Global leadership is not about being the best in the world. It's about being the best for the world."

Robin Sharma

Understanding the Challenges of Regional and Global Roles

Regional and global roles present unique challenges and opportunities for women leaders. These roles often involve managing diverse teams, navigating different cultures, and balancing extensive travel with personal responsibilities.

Women in regional and global roles may face additional pressures to prove their competence and leadership abilities in diverse and often male-dominated environments. The need for cultural sensitivity and adaptability is paramount in these roles.

Balancing extensive travel with family and personal life can be particularly challenging. According to a study by INSEAD, women in global roles often experience higher levels of stress and burnout due to the demands of travel and the complexities of managing remote teams.

Strategies for Success in Regional and Global Roles

Develop cultural intelligence by learning about the cultures and customs of the regions you operate in. This can enhance your effectiveness in managing diverse teams and navigating cross-cultural interactions.

Build a global network by connecting with peers and leaders from different regions. Attend international conferences, join global professional associations, and participate in cross-cultural training programs.

Leverage technology to manage remote teams effectively. Use collaboration tools to facilitate communication and ensure regular check-ins with team members across different time zones.

Plan your travel schedules efficiently to minimize time away from home and maximize productivity. Prioritize self-care during travel by maintaining a healthy routine and managing stress.

Demonstrate flexibility and adaptability in your leadership approach. Understand that different regions may require different leadership styles and strategies. Be open to learning and adjusting your approach based on the cultural context.

Situational Advice

For leaders managing diverse teams, prioritize inclusive communication and foster a culture of mutual respect. Encourage team members to share their perspectives and experiences.

For those balancing extensive travel, create a support system at home to manage personal responsibilities during your absence. Stay connected with family through regular communication and plan quality time together when you are home.

For remote team management, establish clear expectations and accountability. Use virtual collaboration tools to maintain team cohesion and ensure that team members feel supported and valued.

KEY TAKEAWAYS

Cultural Intelligence

Develop an understanding of different cultures and customs.

Global Network

Build connections with peers and leaders from various regions.

Technology

Leverage collaboration tools to manage remote teams.

Efficient Travel

Plan travel schedules to balance productivity and personal life.

Adaptability

Demonstrate flexibility in your leadership approach.

Succeeding in regional and global roles requires cultural intelligence, building a global network, leveraging technology, planning travel efficiently, and demonstrating adaptability. By embracing these strategies, women leaders can thrive in diverse and dynamic environments.

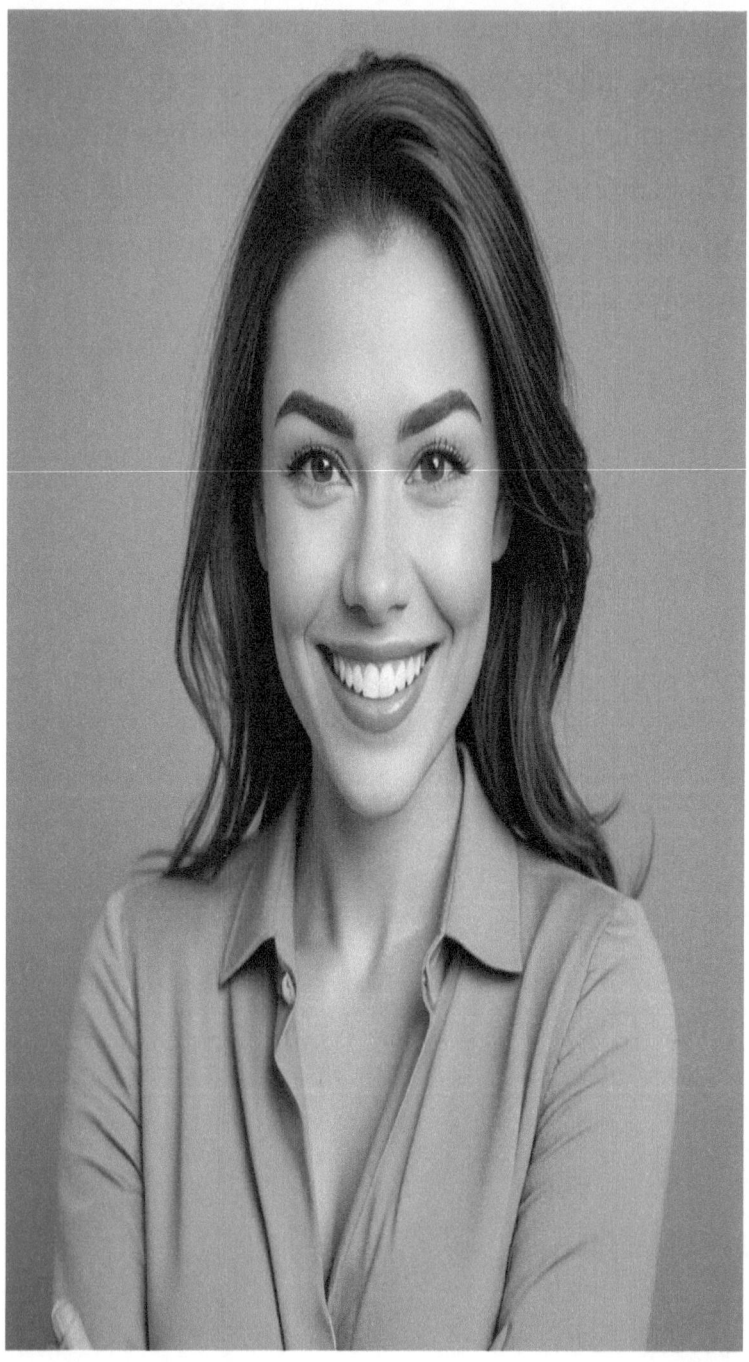

CHAPTER 8

Managing Stress at Work

"You can't pour from an empty cup. Take care of yourself first."

Unknown

Understanding the Stress Challenge

Stress is an inevitable part of leadership, but women often experience it more intensely due to additional pressures and expectations. Managing stress effectively is crucial for maintaining health, productivity, and overall well-being.

According to the American Psychological Association, women are more likely to report physical and emotional symptoms of stress than men. The dual demands of career and personal responsibilities can exacerbate stress levels.

A study by the National Institute for Occupational Safety and Health (NIOSH) found that women report higher levels of job-related stress, which can lead to burnout, anxiety, and other health issues. Managing stress is essential for sustaining long-term career success and personal well-being.

Strategies for Managing Stress

Prioritize self-care by incorporating regular exercise, a healthy diet, and sufficient sleep into your routine. Physical well-being is closely linked to mental health and resilience.

Practice mindfulness and meditation to manage stress and maintain a positive outlook. Techniques such as deep breathing, progressive muscle relaxation, and guided imagery can help reduce stress and promote relaxation.

Establish boundaries between work and personal life. Avoid checking emails or taking work calls during personal time. Creating a clear separation can help you recharge and prevent burnout.

Seek support from peers, mentors, and professional networks. Sharing your experiences and challenges with others can provide emotional support and practical advice. Consider seeking professional help from a therapist or counsellor if needed.

Develop a stress management plan that includes regular breaks, time for hobbies and interests, and activities that bring you joy. Engaging in activities you enjoy can help alleviate stress and enhance your overall well-being.

Situational Advice

For leaders in high-stress environments, identify stress triggers and develop coping strategies. This may include delegating tasks, prioritizing workload, and seeking support from colleagues.

For those balancing remote work, create a structured daily routine that includes regular breaks and time for self-care. Maintain a dedicated workspace to separate professional and personal life.

For on-site roles, take advantage of workplace wellness programs and resources. Participate in stress-relief activities such as yoga, meditation, or fitness classes offered by your organization.

KEY TAKEAWAYS

Self-Care

Prioritize physical and mental well-being through regular exercise, a healthy diet, and sufficient sleep.

Mindfulness

Practice mindfulness and meditation to manage stress.

Boundaries

Establish clear boundaries between work and personal life.

Support

Seek support from peers, mentors, and professional networks.

Stress Management Plan

Develop a plan that includes regular breaks and activities that bring joy.

Managing stress at work is essential for sustaining long-term success and well-being. By prioritizing self-care, practicing mindfulness, establishing boundaries, seeking support, and developing a stress management plan, women leaders can effectively manage stress and thrive in their professional and personal lives.

Chapter 9

The Future of Work for Women

"The future belongs to those who believe in the beauty of their dreams."

Eleanor Roosevelt

Context and Challenges

The future of work is rapidly evolving, shaped by technological advancements, changing demographics, and shifting societal norms. For women leaders, these changes present both opportunities and challenges. Understanding and navigating this dynamic landscape is crucial for staying relevant and advancing in their careers.

According to the World Economic Forum, women are likely to be disproportionately affected by automation and digital transformation. Jobs predominantly held by women, such as administrative and clerical roles, are at high risk of being automated. However, there is also significant potential for women to excel in emerging fields such as technology, artificial intelligence, and sustainable industries.

A report by McKinsey & Company highlights that organizations with greater gender diversity are more likely to outperform their peers. This underscores the importance of fostering inclusive workplaces that leverage the talents of women leaders in shaping the future of work.

Strategies for Thriving in the Future of Work

Embrace Lifelong Learning: Continuous learning and skill development are essential in an ever-changing job market. Women leaders should proactively seek opportunities to upskill and reskill, particularly in high-growth areas such as technology, data analytics, and digital literacy. Online courses, certifications, and professional development programs can provide valuable knowledge and keep skills current.

Leverage Technology: Embrace and leverage technology to enhance productivity and efficiency. Familiarize yourself with digital tools and platforms that facilitate remote work, collaboration, and project management. Understanding and utilizing technology effectively can provide a competitive edge and open new opportunities.

Champion Diversity and Inclusion: Advocate for diversity and inclusion within your organization. Promote policies and practices that support gender equality, such as flexible work arrangements, mentorship programs, and equal pay initiatives. Creating an inclusive culture not only benefits women but also drives innovation and business success.

Develop a Growth Mindset: Adopt a growth mindset, which emphasizes the belief that abilities and intelligence can be developed through dedication and hard work. This mindset encourages resilience, adaptability, and a willingness to embrace challenges. Cultivate a positive attitude towards learning and view setbacks as opportunities for growth.

Expand Your Network: Build and nurture a diverse professional network. Connect with peers, mentors, and industry leaders who can provide support, advice, and opportunities. Participate in industry events, join professional associations, and engage in online communities to expand your network and stay informed about industry trends.

Situational Advice

For Remote Work: Remote work is likely to remain a significant aspect of the future of work. To thrive in a remote environment, establish a dedicated workspace, maintain a structured daily routine, and utilize virtual collaboration tools. Ensure clear communication and set boundaries to balance work and personal life.

For On-Site Roles: On-site roles may require adapting to new health and safety protocols in a post-pandemic world. Stay informed about best practices for workplace safety and be flexible in adapting to changing guidelines. Foster a supportive team environment that prioritizes employee well-being.

For Global Roles: Global roles will increasingly require cultural competence and the ability to navigate diverse work environments. Develop cultural intelligence by learning about different cultures and customs. Use inclusive communication practices and be mindful of time zone differences when working with international teams.

KEY TAKEAWAYS

Lifelong Learning
Continuously seek opportunities to upskill and reskill.

Technology
Embrace and leverage technology to enhance productivity.

Diversity and Inclusion
Champion policies and practices that support gender equality.

Growth Mindset
Cultivate a growth mindset to embrace challenges and setbacks.

As the future of work evolves, women leaders must embrace lifelong learning, leverage technology, champion diversity and inclusion, develop a growth mindset, and expand their networks. By implementing these strategies, women can navigate the challenges and seize the opportunities of the future workplace, ultimately shaping a more inclusive and innovative world.

Chapter 10

Career Progression in the Childbearing Age

"Being a mother has made me so tired. And so happy."

Tina Fey

Context and Challenges

Balancing career ambitions with childbearing and parenting responsibilities is a significant challenge for many women. During the childbearing years, women often face additional hurdles, such as managing pregnancy-related health issues, navigating maternity leave, and balancing childcare responsibilities with professional growth. These challenges can impact career progression and workplace dynamics.

Statistics indicate that many women experience a "motherhood penalty," where they face biases and obstacles that can hinder career advancement. A study by the Harvard Business Review found that mothers are often perceived as less committed to their careers compared to their childless counterparts. However, it's crucial to acknowledge that with the right strategies and support systems, women can successfully navigate this phase and continue to thrive professionally.

Strategies for Thriving During the Childbearing Age

Plan and Communicate: Open communication with your employer and colleagues is essential. Discuss your plans for maternity leave well in advance and create a transition plan to ensure smooth workflow during your absence. Setting clear expectations and timelines can help manage workload and responsibilities effectively.

Leverage Flexible Work Arrangements: Many organizations offer flexible work arrangements, such as remote work, flexible hours, and part-time options. Leverage these arrangements to balance work and family commitments. Flexibility can reduce stress and enable you to maintain productivity while attending to your family's needs.

Build a Support Network: Having a robust support network is invaluable. This includes supportive partners, family members, friends, and professional networks. Don't hesitate to delegate tasks at home and seek help when needed. Networking with other working mothers can provide valuable insights and support.

Focus on Efficiency: Maximize your productivity by focusing on efficient work practices. Prioritize tasks, set realistic goals, and avoid multitasking. Utilize productivity tools and techniques to manage your time effectively. Streamlining your workflow can help you accomplish more in less time.

Seek Mentorship and Sponsorship: Mentorship and sponsorship can play a critical role in your career progression. Seek out mentors who have navigated similar challenges and can offer guidance. Sponsors, who actively advocate for your advancement, can also provide valuable support and opportunities for growth.

Situational Advice

For Remote Work: Remote work can provide the flexibility needed during the childbearing years. Create a structured routine that balances professional and personal responsibilities. Establish clear boundaries to ensure you have dedicated time for work and family.

For On-Site Roles: On-site roles may require additional planning to accommodate pregnancy and childcare needs. Discuss flexible work options with your employer, such as adjusted work hours or telecommuting on certain days. Utilize workplace resources like lactation rooms and parental support programs.

For Global Roles: Global roles often involve travel and irregular hours, which can be challenging during the childbearing years. Communicate with your employer about your travel limitations and seek opportunities for virtual participation in global meetings and projects.

KEY TAKEAWAYS

Planning and Communication
Communicate openly with your employer and plan for maternity leave in advance.

Flexible Work Arrangements
Leverage flexible work options to balance work and family commitments.

Support Network
Build a robust support network to help manage responsibilities at home and work.

Efficiency
Focus on efficient work practices to maximize productivity.

Mentorship and Sponsorship
Seek mentorship and sponsorship to support your career progression.

Navigating career progression during the childbearing years requires planning, flexibility, and a strong support network. By communicating openly, leveraging flexible work arrangements, focusing on efficiency, and seeking mentorship and sponsorship, women can successfully balance their professional ambitions with family responsibilities and continue to advance in their careers.

Chapter 11

Planning Retirement for Women Leaders

"Retirement is not the end of the road. It is the beginning of the open highway."

Unknown

Understanding the Landscape

Planning for retirement is a critical aspect of long-term career and life planning, particularly for women leaders. Women often face unique challenges in retirement planning, including longer life expectancies, potential career interruptions, and the gender pay gap, which can result in lower lifetime earnings and savings. According to a study by the National Institute on Retirement Security, women are 80% more likely than men to be impoverished in retirement.

Despite these challenges, proactive planning and strategic financial management can ensure a secure and fulfilling retirement. It's essential for women leaders to start planning early, stay informed, and make decisions that will safeguard their financial future.

Strategies for Effective Retirement Planning

Start Early and Save Consistently: The earlier you start saving for retirement, the better. Take advantage of employer-sponsored retirement plans, such as 401(k)s or pension schemes and contribute regularly. Utilize compound interest by saving consistently over time. Financial advisors often recommend saving at least 15% of your income towards retirement.

Invest Wisely: Diversify your investments to balance risk and return. Consider a mix of stocks, bonds, and other investment vehicles that align with your risk tolerance and financial goals. Consult with a financial advisor to develop a personalized investment strategy that maximizes growth while managing risk.

Plan for Healthcare Costs: Healthcare expenses can be significant in retirement. Ensure you have adequate health insurance coverage and consider long-term care insurance to cover potential future medical costs. Include these expenses in your retirement planning to avoid unexpected financial burdens.

Understand Social Security Benefits: Familiarize yourself with how Social Security benefits work and the impact of factors such as retirement age and work history on your benefits. Strategize the best time to start drawing benefits to maximize your Social Security income.

Consider Post-Retirement Income: Many women leaders choose to continue working in some capacity during retirement, whether through consulting, part-time work, or starting a new venture. This can provide additional income and keep you engaged and active. Plan for potential post-retirement income sources to supplement your savings.

Situational Advice

For High-Earning Women Leaders: High-earning women should take advantage of additional savings opportunities such as Individual Retirement Accounts (IRAs) and non-qualified deferred compensation plans. Maximize contributions to tax-advantaged accounts and explore investment opportunities that offer higher returns.

For Women with Career Interruptions: Women who have taken career breaks for caregiving or other reasons should focus on catching up on retirement savings. Consider making catch-up contributions to retirement accounts if you are over 50. Explore options such as spousal IRAs to ensure continuous contributions during career interruptions.

For Women in Global Roles: Women in global roles should be aware of the retirement plans and benefits available in different countries. Understand the implications of international work on your retirement savings and ensure you are maximizing benefits across multiple jurisdictions. Consult with financial advisors who specialize in global retirement planning.

KEY TAKEAWAYS

Early and Consistent Saving

Start saving early and contribute regularly to retirement accounts.

Wise Investments

Diversify your investment portfolio to balance risk and return

Healthcare Planning

Plan for healthcare and long-term care costs in retirement.

Social Security Benefits

Understand and strategize Social Security benefits to maximize income.

Post-Retirement Income

Consider opportunities for earning additional income post-retirement.

Retirement planning is a vital component of financial well-being for women leaders. By starting early, investing wisely, planning for healthcare costs, understanding Social Security benefits, and considering post-retirement income opportunities, women can ensure a secure and fulfilling retirement. Taking proactive steps today will pave the way for a comfortable and rewarding future.

The Final Chapter

Embracing Your Leadership Journey

"Leadership is not what you do, it is who you become and how you show up in the world"

Dr Shunitra CS

Reflections on the Path Travelled

As we conclude this exploration of women's leadership, it's essential to reflect on the journey we've navigated together. Leadership, especially for women, is a multifaceted and evolving adventure filled with triumphs, challenges, and invaluable lessons. The chapters in this eBook have aimed to provide insights, strategies, and encouragement to help you thrive as a leader.

The Unique Strengths of Women Leaders

Women bring unique strengths to leadership roles—empathy, collaboration, resilience, and a strong sense of purpose. These qualities not only enhance individual leadership effectiveness but also contribute to more inclusive and innovative organizational cultures. Studies by Harvard Business Review and McKinsey & Company consistently show that diverse leadership teams drive better business performance.

Overcoming Challenges and Embracing Opportunities

The journey of leadership is not without its hurdles. Women often face barriers such as gender bias, work-life balance challenges, and the need to navigate organizational politics. However, as we've discussed throughout this eBook, these challenges can be met with strategic planning, continuous learning, and a supportive network.

Remember the stories and lessons shared in the previous chapters:

- **Balancing Work and Life:** Prioritization, delegation, and setting boundaries are key to maintaining balance.

- **Networking Like a Pro:** Building a strong, diverse network opens doors and provides essential support.
- **Making Decisions with Confidence:** Trusting your instincts and relying on a combination of data and intuition can lead to effective decision-making.
- **Developing and Leading Teams:** Empowering others, fostering collaboration, and promoting a positive culture are hallmarks of effective leadership.
- **Growing Your Career Against All Odds:** Persistence, self-advocacy, and leveraging mentorship and sponsorship are crucial for career advancement.
- **Excelling in Regional and Global Roles:** Cultural intelligence, adaptability, and effective communication are vital for success in international roles.
- **Managing Stress at Work:** Self-care, mindfulness, and resilience-building techniques help maintain well-being in high-pressure environments.

- **The Future of Work for Women:** Embracing technological advancements and advocating for gender equity can shape a promising future.
- **Career Progression in the Childbearing Age:** Strategic planning and supportive workplace policies enable career growth alongside family responsibilities.
- **Planning Retirement for Women Leaders:** Early planning, wise investments, and understanding benefits ensure a secure retirement.

Moving Forward with Confidence and Purpose

As you continue your leadership journey, keep these key takeaways in mind:

- **Self-Awareness and Authenticity:** Leading with self-awareness and authenticity builds trust and inspires others.
- **Lifelong Learning:** Embrace a mindset of continuous learning and growth.

- **Resilience and Adaptability:** Stay resilient in the face of challenges and adaptable to change.
- **Empowerment and Advocacy:** Empower others and advocate for yourself and those around you.
- **Vision and Purpose:** Lead with a clear vision and a strong sense of purpose.

Leadership is a journey, not a destination. It's about making a positive impact, fostering growth in yourself and others, and creating a legacy that inspires future generations. As you move forward, embrace the challenges, celebrate the successes, and never stop striving to be the best leader you can be.

Thank you for joining me on this journey.

It is my sincerest wish that your leadership path be filled with purpose, passion, and endless possibilities. The world needs great women leaders

All images are AI generated from Midjourney

www.imagine.art

www.ingramcontent.com/pod-product-compliance
Lightning Source LLC
Chambersburg PA
CBHW030446220526
45464CB00006B/2430